N nasty Norbert

O an old oak tree

P a piebald pony

Q quivering quills

R a running rabbit

S singing snails

T tongue-tied Tyron

U Uncle Uriah

V a vicious vixen

W a warthog wading in water

X X marks the spot

Y a yawning yak

Z Zack zonking Zeke with a zither

a bevy of bluebirds,
bees, and butterflies

a hippopotamus
in a hot tub

a turtle
taking a
trip

a speeding
snail!

a smiling snake

Cc

crow

cross crows cawing
over a candy cane

candy cane

cow

cow chewing her cud

commode

a cat on a commode

a calico cat trying
to catch
a caged cockatoo

chain

calico cat

cage

cricket

A crocodile
And a cricket
Lost in a thicket.

crocodile

Dd

dog

hat · daisy

duck

fiddle · spoon · Dilly Duck

moon

dish

Dum, diddle diddle
The dog dropped his fiddle,
And this made Dilly Duck swoon.
She fell on the fiddle
Yes, she diddle!
And the dog tossed a dish at the moon!

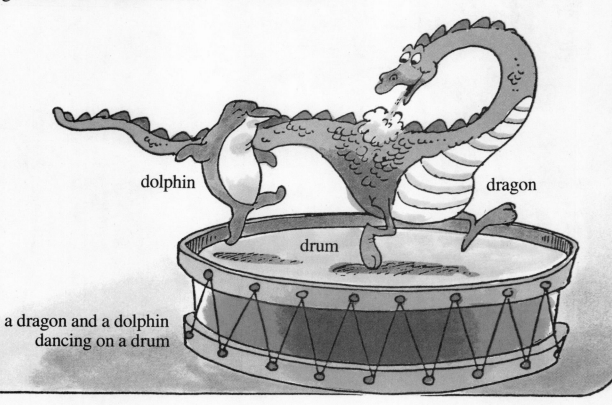

dolphin · dragon

drum

a dragon and a dolphin
dancing on a drum

Ee

Eight elves on an elephant's ear,
Eyeing an egret elegant and clear.
Balanced with ease on one leg,
Standing gently on an egg.

Ff

"Face masks feel funny," said Frank to Fred.

Frank

Fred

fish

Fritz

Said Fritz, when served a fish,
"That's a foul-smelling dish."

fingers

flute

Fat Fonzi Fredo Floo
Keeps his flute in a funky shoe.

Friendly frogs on a pond,
Frolicking midst fern and frond.

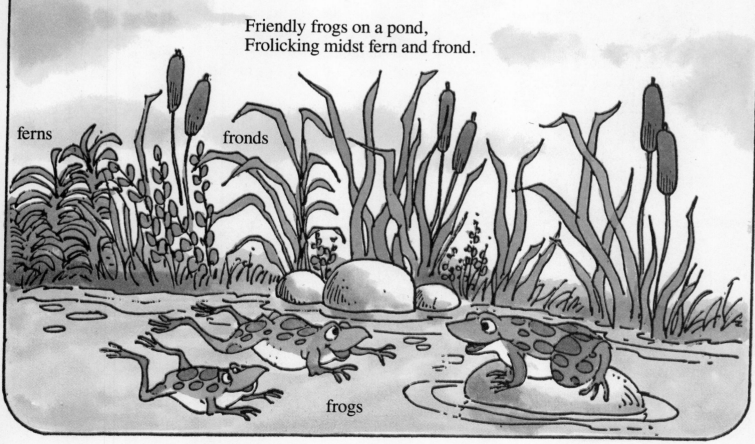

ferns

fronds

frogs

Kk

A koala, a kookaburra and a kinkajou,
Were all trying to learn to play the kazoo.
Finally, along came a kind kangaroo
And showed the trio what to do.

kangaroo

kookaburra

kinkajou

kazoo

koala

kakapos

Kinky King Kakaloka
Of Kakalokataun
Kept two cute kakapos
In his kooky kettle crown.

knights

king

Mm

Merry Marty Munchik and his mini musicians,
Make merry music in his mother's kitchen.

Maxie Mouse
On a mushroom
Balancing two
M's on a broom.

"My, my," said Mother Goose
  To proud Mama Duck.
"What a darling duckling.
  You're so in luck!"

a meeting of musical instruments

Nn

Skinny Nick Ninny fishing on the docks,
Wearing nothing but necktie and socks.

necktie

neck

worms

socks

nuts

nut

nose

A nut fell from a gnarly tree
And knocked Ned on his nose and knee.

Bald Norbert Loggin
Grew a nut tree on his noggin.

Oo

Og

Old Man Mose
Could touch his toes
With his nose.

Og, a dog,
From the planet Zog
Fell to Earth and
Landed on a frog.
Said the frog to Og,
"You bumped my nog."
Said Og to the frog,
"Blame it on the fog."

horns

bull

frog

P p

Peter, Peter, pumpkin eater
Had a wife and couldn't keep her.
He put her in a pumpkin shell.
There she prospered very well.

pumpkin

Peg Leg Pete,
Dresses with flair
He has one leg that
Once adorned a chair.

Pete

pants

Said the proud peacock
To the paltry puffin,
"Compared with me, pal,
You ain't got nothin'."

Peculiar!

a perplexed pelican

Percy Pieman meets Simple Simon.

pocket

A polar bear name Vic
Performing on a pogo stick.

path

Rr

Rupert McGroover is ruder
Than his brother Goober.

bear

pear

rocks

It's a rare bear with
Ne'r a care
That sits on a chair
In his lonely lair
And stares at a pear.

Robert rode around
in his red motor

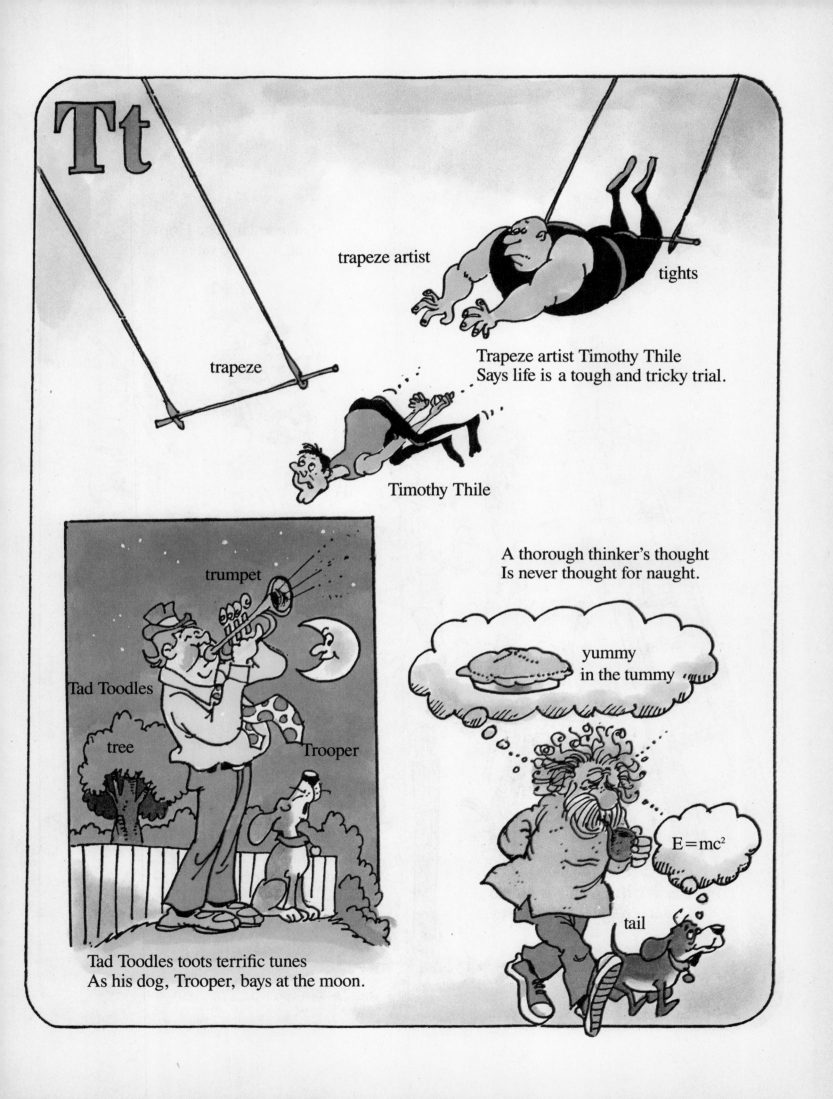

Tt

trapeze artist

tights

trapeze

Trapeze artist Timothy Thile
Says life is a tough and tricky trial.

Timothy Thile

trumpet

Tad Toodles

tree

Trooper

Tad Toodles toots terrific tunes
As his dog, Trooper, bays at the moon.

A thorough thinker's thought
Is never thought for naught.

yummy
in the tummy

$E = mc^2$

tail

Uu

Ubi

upset paint

up

umbrella

Uncle Uria

Uncle Uria and his umbrella
Under a ladder—unlucky fella.

"Unruly," uttered Duke to Ubi Van Horn
Watching Uri ride an untamed unicorn.

Uri

unicorn

Duke

Ursula hanging underwear

underwear

Ursula

Ww

Wanda Witch whipping up some wolfberry stew
For her wandering bats, What, Where, and Who.

Xx

Six foxes with saxophones
Making exquisite musical tones

Yy

On yonder Yazoo Mountain top
Yodeling till his voice would stop,
Stood Yodeler Yussy Yancy Yurt
Yelling for yummy yogurt dessert.

Zz

A zymie, a zonk, and a zawk,
Were out for a morning walk.
They greeted a man
Named Zeke Zacharan
With a polite, "How do you do?"
Said Zeke, who's not meek,
"You belong in a zoo."

A an angry armadillo

B bad boy Bill biting a bee

C carrots doing the cancan

D a dumb dodo

E an excited elf

F a ferocious fish

G a giggling goat

HEE HEE

H a hopping hippopotamus

I an idle ibis

J jabbering jackdaws

K kangaroos playing kazoos

L ladybugs laughing

HA HA

M a mouse on a mushroom